D1087678

101 FACTS ABOUT

GOLDFISH

Please visit our web site at: www.garethstevens.com
For a free color catalog describing Gareth Stevens Publishing's
list of high-quality books and multimedia programs,
call 1-800-542-2595 or fax your request to (414) 332-3567.

Library of Congress Cataloging-in-Publication Data

Barnes, Julia.
   101 facts about goldfish / by Julia Barnes. — North American ed.
     p. cm. — (101 facts about pets)
   Includes bibliographical references and index.
   Summary: Provides information about goldfish, how to care for them,
and how to understand their behavior.
   ISBN 0-8368-3017-2 (lib. bdg.)
   1. Goldfish—Miscellanea—Juvenile literature. [1. Goldfish—Miscellanea.
2. Pets—Miscellanea.] I. Title: One hundred one facts about goldfish.
II. Title. III. Series.
SF458.G6B36   2002
639.3'7484—dc21   2001049752

This North American edition first published in 2002 by
Gareth Stevens Publishing
A World Almanac Education Group Company
330 West Olive Street, Suite 100
Milwaukee, WI 53212 USA

This U.S. edition © 2002 by Gareth Stevens, Inc. Original edition © 2001 by Ringpress Books
Limited. First published by Ringpress Books Limited, P.O. Box 8, Lydney, Gloucestershire,
GL15 4YN, United Kingdom. Additional end matter © 2002 by Gareth Stevens, Inc.

Ringpress Series Editor: Claire Horton-Bussey
Ringpress Designer: Sara Howell
Gareth Stevens Editors: Monica Rausch and Mary Dykstra

Printed in Hong Kong through Printworks Int. Ltd

1 2 3 4 5 6 7 8 9 06 05 04 03 02

101 FACTS ABOUT

GOLDFISH

Julia Barnes

Gareth Stevens Publishing
A WORLD ALMANAC EDUCATION GROUP COMPANY

1 Goldfish are beautiful and interesting pets that are easy to keep. If you are setting up an aquarium for the first time, goldfish may be ideal as your first fish.

2 Keeping goldfish is not a new hobby. The Chinese first bred goldfish more than 1,000 years ago.

3 Early goldfish were dull brown in color and looked like the Crucian Carp, a wild relative of the goldfish.

4 When **breeding** goldfish, the Chinese noticed some of the fish that hatched were gold in color. They placed these fish in a special breeding program.

5 In time, breeders were raising completely orange fish, like the modern goldfish we know today.

6 You can understand and care for your goldfish better if you know how its body works and what the parts of its body are called (below).

7 Goldfish, like all fish, are **cold-blooded**. The body temperature of a goldfish changes with the temperature of the water around it.

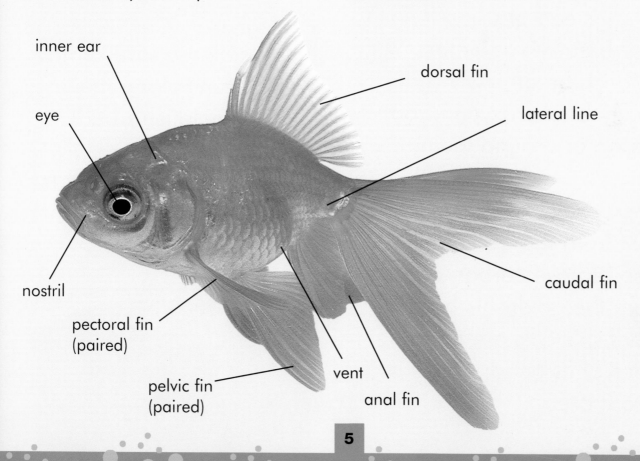

inner ear

eye

nostril

pectoral fin (paired)

pelvic fin (paired)

vent

anal fin

dorsal fin

lateral line

caudal fin

10 A goldfish's body is covered with platelike **scales** that overlap each other. The scales protect the fish from injuries.

8 Instead of using lungs to breathe, as we do, goldfish breathe with **gills**. The gills take oxygen from the water around them.

9 Besides taking oxygen from the water, gills also remove carbon dioxide from the goldfish's body. A goldfish's gills are on the sides of its head, above its throat area.

11 A row of sensors, called a **lateral line** (below), runs along the side of a goldfish's body. The sensors detect, or pick up, movements in the water around the fish.

lateral line

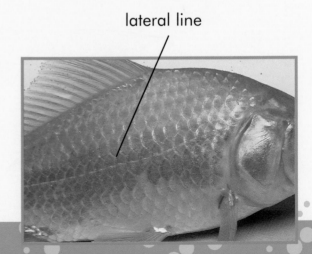

need to sleep, they sink to a low position in the water (below) and do not move. They often turn a paler color so they are harder for predators to see.

12 Goldfish have no eyelids or irises (the colored part of human eyes) so they cannot react quickly to changes in light. Goldfish usually dash for cover, or quickly swim away, when lights are turned on.

13 Because they cannot close their eyes, goldfish have their own way of sleeping. When goldfish

14 A goldfish can see colors and shapes, but not at long distances. A goldfish also can see to the front and sides of its head.

15 Although you cannot see its ears, your goldfish can certainly hear. If you accidentally tap on the aquarium glass, you will see your goldfish dart away in fear.

16 With proper care, most goldfish live for 5 to 10 years, but some varieties of goldfish may live much longer.

17 The oldest goldfish on record was named Fred. Fred lived in West Sussex, England, and lived to be 41 years old.

18 The Common Goldfish (above) has a long, streamlined body with a color that ranges from a deep golden red to a pale yellow gold. Some Common Goldfish also have patches of silver or gold colors on their bodies.

19 Many varieties of goldfish have been bred from the original goldfish. These varieties have many different colors, shapes, and sizes.

20 Goldfish can be grouped into two types: single-tailed varieties and twin-tailed varieties.

21 The Comet (above right) has a very long single tail **fin**, which can be as long or even longer than its body. Comets have slim, streamlined bodies and can swim very quickly.

22 Most Comets are plain yellow in color, but you can also get Comets that have white bodies and bright red coloring along the back.

23 Shubunkins (left), also single-tailed goldfish, are best known for their unusual colors, which include blue-silver, black, red, and violet.

24 London Shubunkins (above) have short fins and thick, stocky bodies. Bristol Shubunkins (below) have more developed, rounded fins. Both types are very colorful.

25 Goldfish with twin tail fins have shorter bodies than single-tailed types. Some varieties of twin-tailed goldfish do not swim well.

26 The Fantail (below) has a rounded body and flowing double tail fins. Fantails swim quite well and are some of the easiest twin-tailed goldfish to keep.

27 The Veiltail has a flowing tail that hangs in folds. The fin on a Veiltail's back, called the dorsal fin, is very tall. These fish can easily hurt themselves on rough, sharp objects.

28 Although the Moor (above) is a goldfish, it is always black in color. Moors have eyes that stick out from the sides of their heads, like little telescopes.

29 The Ryukin has a short, heavy body; a steeply curved back; and flowing fins. When seen from behind, a Ryukin resembles a butterfly. Despite its **fancy** appearance, the Ryukin is surprisingly **hardy**.

30 The Lionhead (below) is a poor swimmer because it does not have a dorsal fin. Lionheads have egg-shaped bodies and raspberrylike growths on their heads.

31 The Oranda also has a growth on its head, but an Oranda has a dorsal fin. The Red-capped Oranda has a white body and a red cap on top of its head. Orandas sometimes are called "gooseheads."

33 Fancy goldfish are bred for their looks, rather than for the health and well-being of the fish, and they are more difficult to care for. They are not a good choice if you are setting up your first fish tank.

32 There are many other unique and wonderful types of goldfish. The Bubble-eye (above) has large fluid-filled sacs under its eyes, and the Pompom (below) has cheerleaderlike pompoms growing near its nostrils.

34 Before you buy your goldfish, you need to set up a suitable home for your new pets. Tanks come in many different shapes and sizes and are made of a variety of materials.

36 It is best to choose a glass tank, since plastic tanks tend to scratch. The tank should have a lid, called a hood, fitted on top.

37 For a basic aquarium set up for goldfish, you will need gravel for the bottom of the tank. You also can have some plants and rocks.

35 Goldfish need a lot of oxygen, which they get from the water, so a large rectangular tank is an ideal home for them. In general, you should have 1 gallon (3.8 liters) of water for each 1 inch (2.5 centimeters) of fish. For one goldfish, you will need a 10-gallon (38-liter) tank.

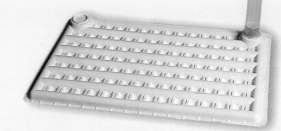

38 An aquarium needs a **filter** to keep the tank clean. Like all living animals, fish need to get rid of waste from their bodies. The filter breaks down the fish's waste so it becomes harmless.

39 Two basic types of filters are used in aquariums. A box filter (below right) can be hung inside or outside of the tank.

40 An undergravel filter (above) is a filter that fits across the bottom of the tank, under the gravel.

41 Filters are powered by electricity. You can buy a variety of filters at any pet store that sells fish.

44 Too much sunlight will cause **algae** to grow on the sides of the aquarium.

42 Lighting your tank will help you see your goldfish more clearly. You can buy a hood for your tank that has a light fitted into it. Most light hoods use fluorescent bulbs, which help plants grow inside the tank.

45 Your aquarium will be very heavy when it is full of water, so be sure it is sitting on a table strong enough to support it.

46 If you are using lighting or a filter, you need to place the tank close to an electrical outlet.

43 Do not place your aquarium in constant, direct sunlight.

15

printed with exotic scenes of marine life. The choice is yours!

47 The most fun part of setting up your aquarium is deciding how it is going to look. Your goal is to provide a healthy home that also looks great!

48 Start with a backing sheet that attaches to the side of the tank. Some backing sheets are all one color, while other sheets are

49 You need a gravel surface in your aquarium. You can buy brightly colored gravel or choose gray or tan gravel for a more natural look.

50 Goldfish like having places to hide. Rocks and ornaments (below) may provide great hiding places.

putting them into the tank. Check with an expert fishkeeper at a pet store to make sure the materials are suitable for a goldfish tank.

51 You can choose from a variety of aquarium ornaments, from scuba divers and shipwrecks to fantasy castles that create a magical kingdom. Let your imagination go wild as you set up your tank.

53 Plants add color and variety to a tank. Goldfish enjoy swimming among the plants, which provide hiding places, and nibbling on them.

52 Shells and rocks (above) provide a more natural look inside a tank. Be sure to wash all of these materials well before

54 Several types of aquatic, or water, plants do well in a goldfish aquarium.

55 Many pet stores sell Java Fern (below left), Sagittaria (also known as "arrowheads"), and Water Milfoil (below right) for use in fish tanks.

56 After buying the equipment you need, plus the plants and ornaments, you are ready to set up the aquarium for your goldfish.

57 Wash the gravel under running water before putting it into the tank.

58 Cover the bottom of the tank with gravel, and make a gentle slope from the back of the tank to the front. If you are using an undergravel filter, you need to put it in place before adding the gravel (top right).

18

in your tank, you must let it stand for three days before adding your goldfish, to remove the **chlorine** that is present in tap water.

59 If you are using a box filter, you should attach the filter to the side of the tank.

60 Next, wash the ornaments and rocks and position them in the tank.

61 Now you can fill the tank with water. If you use ordinary tap water

64 After your tank is set up, you can buy your goldfish. Purchase your fish at a good pet store that has an experienced staff to give you advice.

62 You can also add special solutions to the water to remove the chlorine and any metals from the water.

65 Fish can suffer from stress if their tank is overcrowded, so choose your fish from a tank where the fish look active and healthy.

63 If you have live plants for your aquarium, add them before you fill the tank (top).

66 The pet store staff should be able to answer your questions and help you make your choice.

67 When choosing your fish, look for the following signs of good health (below).

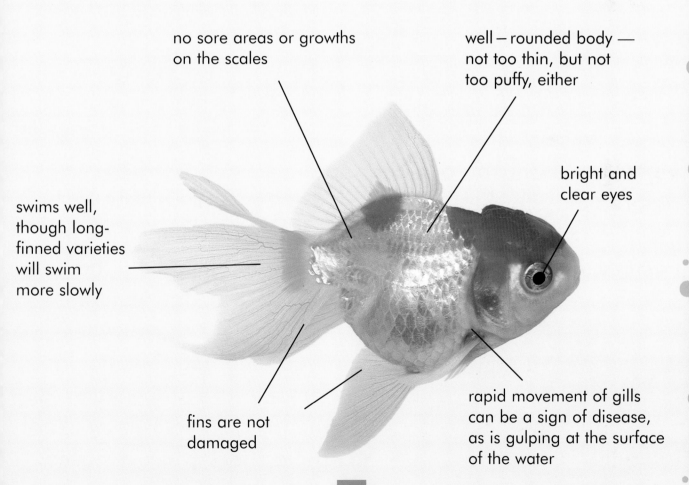

no sore areas or growths on the scales

well – rounded body — not too thin, but not too puffy, either

bright and clear eyes

swims well, though long-finned varieties will swim more slowly

fins are not damaged

rapid movement of gills can be a sign of disease, as is gulping at the surface of the water

68 Do not mix slower-swimming, fancy types of goldfish, such as Fantails, with singled-tailed varieties, such as Comets.

69 Even if you have a large tank, it is better to start off with just a few goldfish. You can add more goldfish when you are confident that your aquarium is functioning properly.

70 The fish you choose will be caught in a net and put into a plastic bag filled with water so you can safely carry them home.

71 When you get home, do not put your goldfish directly into the tank.

72 Instead, put the bag into your tank (top right) and let it float there for 20 minutes. You want the temperature of the water inside the bag to equal the temperature of the water in the tank, so your fish will not get a shock when released.

75 Your fish may come to the surface to feed or find the food at the bottom of the tank (below), as the food settles on the gravel.

73 Give your goldfish a chance to get used to their new surroundings before giving the fish their first meal in their beautiful new home.

76 The biggest mistake made by some first-time fish owners is overfeeding their pets. Uneaten food decomposes, or breaks down, in the water and can make your fish sick.

74 A wide range of dried food can be bought for goldfish. Goldfish food usually comes in flake form and provides your fish with all the **nutrients** they need.

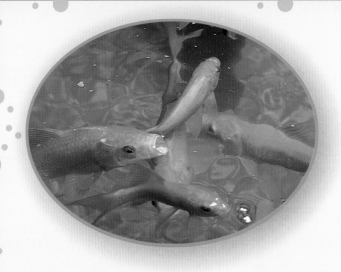

79 If you want to give your goldfish a treat, buy some daphnia, also called fleas, from your local pet store. Only buy a small quantity of daphnia, so they all get eaten at one time.

77 Feed your fish only as much as they will eat within 2 minutes. Goldfish need to be fed twice a day.

78 Try to feed your fish at the same time each day, once in the morning and once at night.

80 Once you have set up your tank, it is quite easy to keep it running. You will need to change part of the water on a regular basis, however, to keep your tank clean and healthy.

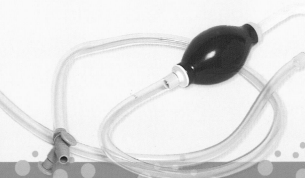

81 In a tank without a filter, replace 10 to 20 percent of the water twice a week. In a tank with a filter, replace this amount of water every few weeks. To remove the dirty water, use plastic tubing, called a **siphon**.

82 Dip the siphon in the water to fill it, then place a finger over both ends. Put one end of the tube in the bottom of the tank and the other end in a bucket below the level of the tank. Release your fingers. The water will begin to flow into the bucket.

83 Take the tubing out of the tank as soon as you have removed enough water.

84 Before filling your tank with fresh water, allow the new water to stand for two hours or add a conditioner to it that removes chlorine before adding the water to your aquarium.

85 Algae is not harmful to goldfish, but it may spoil the look of your aquarium when it grows on the sides of your tank.

86 Use an algae scraper, which can be purchased at a pet store, to clean the inside walls of your aquarium every two to three weeks (below).

87 Goldfish can get a number of different health problems. It is important to spot possible signs of trouble early so you can seek the help of a veterinarian or an expert in fish care.

88 If you spend time watching your fish, you will probably notice if something is wrong with it.

89 If a fish is sick, it may stop eating. If a fish doesn't eat, its body may appear too thin or it may look swollen.

90 Sometimes when a fish is sick, it swims in an unusual way or gasps at the surface of the water.

91 A fish suffering from stress may hold its fins very close to its body.

92 To keep your fish healthy, look for lumps or swellings on its skin and any injuries to its fins.

93 If you think your fish is sick or injured, go to a pet store to find out about medicated food or possible treatments that can be added to the water.

94 Goldfish are usually only **aggressive** during the breeding season, which takes place in spring or summer. At this time, females lay eggs that are fertilized by male fish.

95 The breeding season is the only time you can tell male and female goldfish apart. A female's body (above right) becomes swollen with eggs. The male (above left) may develop white spots over its gills and on its front fins.

96 The female lays a batch of eggs that are the size of tiny pinheads on plants in the tank.

97 For the eggs to hatch, they need to be placed in a special **hatchery** tank. If left in the regular tank, the adult fish will eat the eggs.

98 The hatchery tank should be kept at a temperature of around 70° Fahrenheit (21° Celsius). The eggs hatch in four or five days.

101 Breeding goldfish is difficult to do and is best left to experts. You will find, however, that setting up an aquarium and caring for fascinating goldfish is a great hobby, and, in time, you may become a fish expert, too!

99 The young fish, known as **fry**, look like tiny hairs attached to the plants in the fish tank.

100 After about three days, the fry start swimming around the tank. They need special fry food, sold at pet stores, to develop into healthy adults.

Glossary

aggressive: quick to attack or start a fight.

algae: tiny water plants that do not have roots, stems, or leaves.

breeding: raising particular varieties of a species of animal.

chlorine: a chemical added to the water we drink and use, which is harmful to fish.

cold-blooded: having a body temperature that changes with the temperature of the surrounding environment.

fancy: describing types of goldfish bred for their unique appearance.

filter: a machine used to break down waste products in water.

fin: a thin, flat part sticking out from the body of a fish. Fish use fins for movement and balance.

fry: young fish.

gills: the parts on a fish's body used to take oxygen out of water.

hardy: able to stay healthy under a variety of conditions.

hatchery: a tank used for hatching fish eggs, in which no adult fish are allowed.

lateral line: a line of sensors along the side of a fish's body that detect movement in the water.

nutrients: ingredients in food that nourish an animal and provide what is needed for development.

scales: small, thin, platelike parts covering a fish's body.

siphon: a piece of tubing in which air pressure forces water to flow from one container to another, lower container.

More Books to Read

Goldfish (Fish and Aquariums series) Spencer Glass (Chelsea House)

Goldfish (Pets series) Michaela Miller (Heinemann Library)

My Goldfish Pam Walker (Children's Press)

Taking Care of Your Goldfish Helen Piers (Barron's Educational)

Web Sites

Goldfish information www.geocities.com/Heartland/ Hills/5086/care.htm

Goldfish World www.angelfire.com/wy/kokopalee

Goldfish Guy www.goldfishguy.com

Goldfish care www.cyber-dyne.com/~Nunnie/ goldfish.html

To find additional web sites, use a reliable search engine, such as www.yahooligans.com, with one or more of the following keywords: **goldfish, pet fish, aquarium, lionhead, oranda**.

Index